# BWAY

## BY ALEX SUMMERS

Rourke
Educational Media
rourkeeducationalmedia.com

Scan for Related Titles
and Teacher Resources

**Teaching Focus:**
Concepts of Print: Have students find capital letters and punctuation in a sentence. Ask students to explain the purpose for using them in a sentence.

## Before Reading:

### Building Academic Vocabulary and Background Knowledge

Before reading a book, it is important to set the stage for your child or student by using pre-reading strategies. This will help them develop their vocabulary, increase their reading comprehension, and make connections across the curriculum.

1. Read the title and look at the cover. *Let's make predictions about what this book will be about.*
2. Take a picture walk by talking about the pictures/photographs in the book. Implant the vocabulary as you take the picture walk. Be sure to talk about the text features such as headings, the Table of Contents, glossary, bolded words, captions, charts/diagrams, or Index.
3. Have students read the first page of text with you then have students read the remaining text.
4. Strategy Talk – use to assist students while reading.
   - Get your mouth ready
   - Look at the picture
   - Think…does it make sense
   - Think…does it look right
   - Think…does it sound right
   - Chunk it – by looking for a part you know
5. Read it again.

**Content Area Vocabulary**
*Use glossary words in a sentence.*

connect
operator
rails
station

## After Reading:

### Comprehension and Extension Activity

After reading the book, work on the following questions with your child or students in order to check their level of reading comprehension and content mastery.

1. *What do trains and subways have in common? (Summarize)*
2. *What is the person who drives the subway called? (Asking Questions)*
3. *Have you ever ridden anything like a subway? (Text to self connection)*
4. *When the benches are full on a subway car, what do you hold on to? (Asking Questions)*

### Extension Activity

Subways and Trains. With the help of an adult, divide a piece of paper in half. On one side write the word Trains. On the other side write the word Subways. Now, discuss the things trains and subways have in common. List them on your paper. Next, discuss the differences between trains and subways and list those on your paper. Are they more different or more alike?

# Table of Contents

# Underground Ride

Ready to go!

How will I get there?

I know! I will take a subway. The subway **station** is underground.

subway

There are lots of people waiting to board. The subway arrives. The doors open.

A subway looks like a train. It has no wheels. It runs on **rails**.

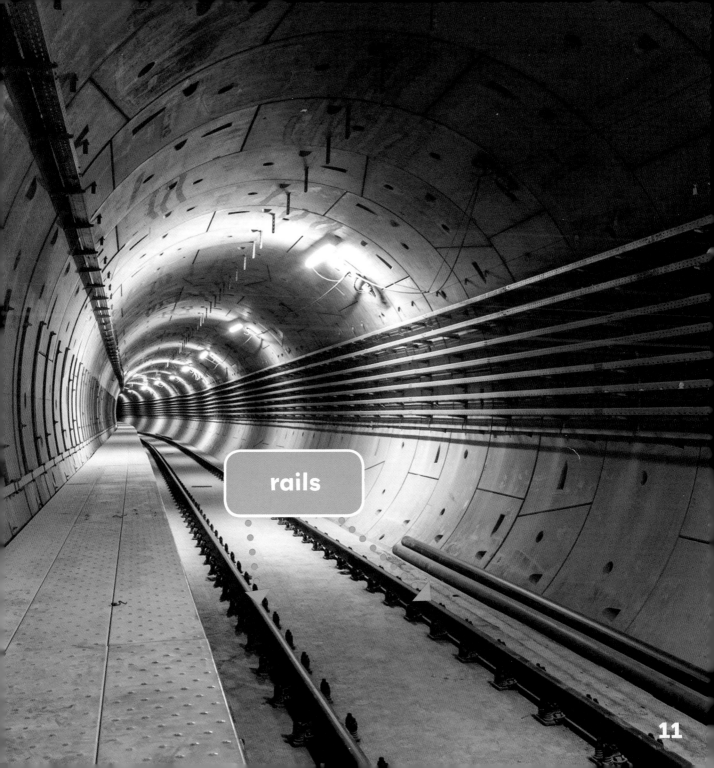

rails

# Inside a Subway Car

There are benches inside. People hold on to poles in the middle.

poles

Dozens of subway cars **connect** together. An **operator** at the front drives.

connect

operator

The subway goes fast!
It is dark outside
the windows.

# Subway Stations

There are many subway stations. People get on and off at each one.

**Chambers Street Station**

Ⓙ Ⓩ ④ ⑤ ⑥

♿ Elevator to ④⑤⑥ at
Centre St & Chambers St

Enter with or buy MetroCard at
all times or see agent at
Chambers St & Centre St

19

The subway stops.
The operator calls the
name of the station.

The doors open
and off I go!

# Picture Glossary

 **connect** (kuh-NEKT): When you connect something, you join it to something else.

 **operator** (AH-puh-ray-tur): Someone who works a machine or device, such as a subway.

 **rails** (rayls): Fixed bars supported by posts that allow a subway to stay on a track.

 **station** (STAY-shuhn): A place where tickets for trains and subways are sold.

# Index

# Websites to Visit

https://mommypoppins.com/ny-kids/a-kids-guide-to-new-york-underground-subways-and-beyond

www.parkslopeparents.com/Tween-Advice-from-Parents/roadmap-for-independence-kids-riding-the-subway

www.pinterest.com/tahnee_b/subway-art-ideas

# About the Author

Alex Summers enjoys all forms of transportation. Especially if they are taking her to places she has never been or seen before. She loves to travel, read, write, and dream about all the places she will visit someday!

**Meet The Author!**
www.meetREMauthors.com

**Library of Congress PCN Data**

Subway / Alex Summers
(Transportation and Me!)
ISBN 978-1-68342-165-8 (hard cover)
ISBN 978-1-68342-207-5 (soft cover)
ISBN 978-1-68342-234-1 (e-Book)
Library of Congress Control Number: 2016956607

Rourke Educational Media
Printed in the United States of America,
North Mankato, Minnesota

**Also Available as:**

© 2017 Rourke Educational Media

www.rourkeeducationalmedia.com

Edited by: Keli Sipperley
Cover design by: Tara Raymo
Interior design by: Rhea Magaro-Wallace
Photo Credits: Cover: ©hellena13; ©400tmax; page 5a, 6, 22: ©Samuel Borges Photography; page 5b: ©Pogonici; page 5c: ©Nerthuz; page 7: ©ellisonphoto; page 9: ©Allen G.; page 11: ©Olive Sved; page 13: ©Rusian Dashinsky; page 15: ©baranozdemir; page 17: ©Uatap1; page 19: ©deberarr; page 21: ©golgachov; page 22: ©Lena Ivanov